Good Holding Ground

Good Holding Ground

Palimpsest Press
5 King St, Kingsville, Ontario, Canada N9Y 1H9
www.palimpsestpress.ca

Book and cover design by Dawn Kresan. Typeset in Adobe Garamond Pro,
and printed offset on Rolland Zephyr Laid at Coach House Printing.

Library and Archives Canada Cataloguing in Publication

Woodman Kerkham, Cynthia
Good holding ground / Cynthia Woodman Kerkham.

Poems.
ISBN 978-1-926794-05-1

        I. Title.
        PS8645.O6384G66 2011
        C811'.6   C2011-900879-3

We thank the Canada Council for the Arts and the Ontario Arts Council for
their support of our publishing program.

CONTENTS

I. Good Holding Ground

II. Tattoo

III. Leaving the Body

IV. In the Night Sky, A Crab

I

Good Holding Ground

LATE SUMMER IN FREDERICK ARM

They call all experience of the senses 'mystic', when the experience is considered.
So an apple becomes mystic when I taste in it
the summer and the snows, the wild welter of earth
and the insistence of the sun.
          —DH Lawrence "Mystic"

Here at the head of the crucifix, Frederick Arm
flows into Nodales Channel; Cordero is the crosspiece.
A week anchored at a half-drowned dock,
Frederick was a British explorer, but the name
is known to me from a child's tale of a mouse
who spends his hours slow-gathering nuts and noticing
the gauze of dusk's mayfly over the lake's smooth cheek.
His neighbours scurry about their work;
chastise Frederick's laziness; make their disapproval heard.
They call all experience of the senses 'mystic', when the experience is considered.

The Frederick in me wonders this morning how to translate
the preening of herring gulls lined on a log—
chatter of croaks and caws, tweets and quacks
that must be about fish, and the obstinacy of tick under wing.
Into silence comes the click of alder leaves as they tumble gold
amongst evergreen; the skritch of gravel on abandoned logging roads;
a rockslide's distant, throaty rumble.
How know we are alive if not in the noticing?
In an abandoned orchard, sit.
So an apple becomes mystic when I taste in it

the drip of glaciers, granite dust
and tart sun. Or in the flesh
of Esturo Basin trout the taste
of water grasses, sweet lake, a dusting of sea.
I soak in this elemental place:
its lightness of spirit and aura of limitless days.
Float in the wild silence where all the Fredericks
can stretch their reach beyond the business of living;

can pull into eyes' and lungs' full girth,
the summer and the snows, the wild welter of earth.

Each hour skims magic
like phosphorescence in a night sea.
Here senses rule. And Fredericks
store their visions for the telling in the long winters,
when the seeds are nearly spent,
when the dark cave closes in,
and trapped mice seek the value
of experience considered; then Frederick will rise,
recount tug of unfurling leaf, green smell of ocean,
and the insistence of the sun.

SUDS

I don't drink beer but love the suds mustache
that forms above my husband's upper lip

when, after a hot day he'll quaff a glass.
I have a dozen in the trunk as I reverse into the narrow

Thrifty Food parking lot lane. I don't see the man coming, am sure
I've checked, but he's swung his small red truck around the bend

just as I look the other way. Whatever. He's certain
it's my fault that we've nearly collided and flings

the universal sign of disapproval. I toss one back;
not in anger but in jest, a part of my brain watching itself

gesticulate with zest. All in good comedy, I think,
until he slams into park, leaps from his cab

and charges at my driver's window which I rapidly close.
Head bent, from the corner of my eye

I see spittle fly like suds as he curses me
to a growing audience. Like the time my husband

sat alone at a bar in Colorado sipping beer, and a hand thudded
on his shoulder, swung him round on the revolving stool

and fisted into his face. The barman leapt over his bar,
his feet landing squarely on the farmer's chest.

You're lucky you didn't fight back, the policeman said after it was all over,
the hippie last week did and he's still in hospital with knife wounds.

The man in the red truck gets back in his cab and makes to ram
the passenger side of my car, inches forward, revs, inches forward

11

pins me in and continues to scream through his open window
sexual words meant to mutilate. I close my eyes and meditate

which revs him even higher. As luck would have it
two police stand by the liquour store

selling buttons for muscular dystrophy
and someone runs to fetch them. I roll my window down

for the policewoman who sees my shaking hands and asks
if I'm OK to drive. My husband is at the kitchen table, drinking a beer.

He pulls me onto his lap. My finger trembles as I reach
to swipe his upper lip clean of suds, marvel at their evanescence.

FRIENDSHIP HAS FRIGHTENED ME

The sign at the entrance to the Box Canyon hike
reads: Beware the Plague. Stay away
from rats, their desiccated bodies, gorged fleas.
An ancient fear of communal disease,
of shunning and shipping the afflicted,
rises in the desert heat.

But we decide to risk it.
Our conversation swings
as lightly as if we were holding hands.
New to this landscape,
we present it as a gift to the other
calling in the voices of children
as we signpost the colours of desert bloom
rising from the rain—yellow knobs
of cacti, cornflower blues,
Indian paintbrush, its sunrise orange.

And the cliffs! The cliffs!
Like God's molars, you say.
Like ruined temples, I reply.
You twist an ankle on a stone,
I catapult my head into an overhang;
we pause and help each other
follow the spurned river to its source,
arriving at water. Its fall and pooling,
its hope-song
in all this forsaken dryness.

PADDLING ON TOP OF THE WORLD

*The look between animal and man has been extinguished…this historic
loss, to which zoos are a monument, is now irredeemable for the culture
of capitalism.*
　　　　　—John Berger, "Why Look at Animals?"

What would we have done if an elk
in this rutting season had come
to the river's edge, and bellowed
in our always fearful ears?

Come to the river's edge where we dig
our paddles out of the wind—the Bow River,
silt green and muscled, the Irishwoman
in the bow, virgin canoeist. I teach her

a camp song: *My paddle's keen and bright,*
a round that dissolves in laughter. She teaches me
a Gaelic air I cannot pronounce,
something about paddling home.

We try to feel at home in this wilderness,
groomed for us with rented blue canoes,
red life-jackets, and we fall into quiet
strokes, searching the park shores for animals.

Another boat in our group returns
with reports of horse sightings.
Tame but beautiful, no doubt;
and this setting of yellow grass and fen

makes it easier to imagine wild.
Only the heron takes us to a liquid prehistoric
where once we were animal,
seeing our place in the eyes of elk.

We are disappointed but content
to report on tame horses,
the heron's heavy flight
then distant blink.

OMEN

The moment we met at Athens airport,
we kissed, made love that humid night—
your lover, my best friend
had told me to stay away from you.

We kissed, made love that humid night
at the Agapemou Hotel, breath oily with retsina
her voice saying stay away from you
coming into the harbour at Chania

from the Agapemou Hotel, breath oily with retsina
we were in love, and not;
coming into the harbour at Chania
a full moon rising as the sun descended

we were in love, and not
a perfect paradox, day-night sky
a full moon rising as the sun descended
we were air and light, blue and white

a perfect paradox, day-night sky
born with the seeds of its own demise
we were air and light, blue and white
with no good earth beneath us

born with the seeds of our own demise
bright mornings, rucked sheets
with no good earth beneath us
browned bodies entwined

bright mornings, rucked sheets
brandied evenings, leaving fidelity undefined
browned bodies entwined
shrouded in clouds of desire

brandied evenings, leaving fidelity undefined
you saw a woman from our balcony
shrouded in clouds of desire
you called her perfect, too.

You saw a woman from our balcony,
long legs draped in harem pants
you called her perfect, too; we were
addicts to romance

that night yellow faded out of clear blue
remembering your lover, my best friend,
the way I lost myself
the moment we met at Athens airport.

AFTER THE ABORTION

The counselor sits beside her hospital bed
surprised at her cheerfulness,
as everyone is.

A year after the lover has gone,
she's doing dishes;
on the radio, an informative program:

a foetus at four months,
(bud hands, leaf cheek)
can feel a feather's tip.

Her knees buckle.
Who is making that animal sound?

WEEDING

I cup it in my hand
try not to count its tiny buds

plucked out. Something I'd planted
now bound for a bag of refuse.

Perhaps I knew
it would never bloom for me.

Today, when I heard your name
my heart rose

and I can't stop myself
imagining

your flowering.

DEADFALL

Logs like deer under clear water
their burnt black knots stare

accusing from the aching cold
      buried strength

slick limbs stretched full length

patches of white where light
tunnels
      through
          sea

a stag   antlers huge
shrouded
in green algae

     slimed legs locked with the female
fallen in a final embrace   arbutus bodies
smooth as the unborn

 ashamed

    waterlogged

I've traveled too long with regret.

FALLING IN LOVE WITH THE POTTER

Some trouble took her to this job,
making glazes in a clapboard pottery shed
its wood a brick red from years
of storm scouring. The potter
in his basement studio,
hands mud-wet and worn
to a baby softness by clay grit.
She was a woman freighted
with many loves gone
and the potter knew his own grief.
The thrum of his wheel carried
through winter mist,
through the summer's kiln-dried air.
Glints of amber in her tied-back hair
as she weighed kaolin and iron oxide,
manganese and cobalt. The sound of her breathing
steady and muted behind the white mask,
skin dusted in clay flour,
luster of bone ash and flint,
skim of sweat glossing her upper lip.
The tiny brass weights poised on scales,
delicate balance where one gram, like a choice,
could make a world of difference,
make a glaze stick and shine wet
and waxy, or slide and puddle hard
blister, craze or crawl.
Sometimes the potter called
with tea and they'd sit in the dandelioned yard.
He'd tell stories of Shoji Hamada,
separated from them by an ocean and a generation;
but his craft so close on those pre-dawn openings,
the first glimpse of vases, platters and bowls,
the blaze of things made
in oil-spot tenmoku or blue-green celadon—
such colours unearthed—ox-blood copper, amber slip.

MARRIAGE SUITE

Beginnings: That first summer
lime lily leaves on a sage lake
the mint of morning air.

Afternoons we lay
on the hot dock boards
sniffed the honey of baked pine.

All business stopped
but for the patient work of linked bodies.
August-browned. We swam

in the night lake, tipped white bottoms
to the moon. Lay in cedar rooms
breathing green.

*

Remembering Past Lovers: Oh,
to have a Lee Valley Dandelion Digger,
to go below the root,
eradicate these blights,
on our morning landscape.

*

First Years: I kick you once,
you steel-toe boot me back.

November in the woods and the mushrooms
knuckle their way through earth,
colour of toenail, of blood blister.
Domes drenched in champagne rains
like boxers' gloves glisten.
Tough little pugilists
steeped in the art of becoming.

*

Digging: day and night in the garden,
and my nails are chipped and filled with dirt,
my fingers dry.
Friends say, *You look worn out.*

That's how hard this marriage seems to me.

*

When You Don't Listen: I feel
like a sheet of beaten tin
into which you gaze
at your reflection.

*

You Take Me Away for My Birthday: my mind
feels only muscles,
their unruffling,

and the flutter from eyelid of an afternoon closed
like the sign flipped on a shop's glass door—

silent shelves
dimmed interior

and you, the animal lying beside me.

*

Ten Year Anniversary: Work and love
and sex that nudges
between our legs
like a dog welcoming
us home.

*

Alone / Together: Outside our island window
a robin sings from pink arbutus
skinned raw green
clear call
of morning
so deep
we fall
and find
ourselves everywhere.

*

Darling, Nature's had its way with me.
Now I'm free
to dry up
spawned.

*

*Why the Night-Blooming Cereus
only Shows Itself in the Dark.* That night
I shrank to a single cell
turned my back,
spooned away.

You snugged your palm on my shoulder.
How like the Night-Blooming Cereus
I turned to your light, lips parting
like the sheaths of lunar flowers,
teeth, gleaming white petals.

PREGNANT

On the back of bathroom stalls
salacious animal words suddenly delicious.
I waddle to the store, buy erotic magazines,
read titillating stories in a private corner of the park:
how Rod lusts after what Sylvie does with her dog.
What is wrong with me?
I swell through summer into the third trimester,
swim evenings in the local pool, and after lengths,
soak in the shallow kiddie's pond,
glowing fecundity. Men try to pick me up
until I rise, my grand womb an inch
from their startled noses.
But I don't blame them. I want sex all the time,
devour my husband who's worried but willing
until, at last, the pod bursts
the baby born and I dissolve
into showers of milk.

WHAT TO SAY

After twenty years you write to tell me you love me.
Back home I weed my imperfect garden,
lovely to me the montbretia leaves—
a bristle of blades, the mallow now
popping pink trumpets.
Your ghost still alive
hisses of bed sheets,
of my perfect young body you called
the yacht. My husband
is down at the dock, working
on his imperfect boat,
lovely to him the clump of wires
he has unwoven, the sail
he has repaired. He will take us
up the coast to swim in warm fjords
after a winter of hard work, I will hold
a party in the garden.
I don't know what to say to you.
I loved your perfection, too. Dream
of meeting it again. But we forget
how we destroyed such flawlessness.
Your memory, like mine, imperfect.

WE MAKE A DIFFERENT LOVE THIS MORNING

How subtle is the sex of graveyard trees—
chestnut's candle, its creamy blossomed froth,
blood blush on petal sheet; hopeful pistils.
Pine strobili rise from curly ovules,
their sex a bundle of female-male where
each wax-green needle lies embedded in
a flesh-coloured bract ready to burst bright—
an inch of new lime on old emerald.
We start a new Spring after child-rearing.
This morning sex full of history—a
yes to all the years we've spent together
and yes to more. We enter a wellspring
      beyond the fever of firsts. We know curled
      leaf hugs branch tip before it can unfurl.

GOOD HOLDING GROUND

We pull into harbour
perform ceremonies
of forward and reverse.
Husband on the bow
I'm at the wheel,
both alert to see
if the anchor has set
or slips on seaweed,
sand or shale.
Always after anchoring
a post-coital moment—
we eat apples
in the cockpit
toss the cores overboard
to the waiting loveless gulls.
One more check for no chafing
lines secure, we go below to bed
to float in dreamy sashays

grateful this marriage holds.

HANGING LAUNDRY

We're sailing past Texada Island
down Georgia Strait on a hot, flat day.
I'm hanging laundry on the jib sheet.
My husband stands braced
against the navy bimini,
binoculars focused.
The miners have made
an open-faced sandwich
of the mountain. Its filling
spilling out, gobbled up by Tonka trucks.
In an abandoned logging camp up the coast,
they'd scrawled the names of blast sites
on a whiteboard—Gynecology Cut
and Whores Run.
Yesterday at Lund, loggers
roared up to the gas dock,
jumped out of their aluminum boat
slammed down the gas lever,
stalked about with their smokes,
put the bill on the tab,
clambered in and gunned off.
They filled their boat
with three times the fuel
while the hose in my hand
hung limp and dripping.
Patch logging like scabies
up and down the coastal skin.
I had sex with a miner,
lust that lasted about as long
as a virgin forest, as long as
a gold mountain in a mining town.
The sea flows by in silken cords.
Will the dust from the quarry
blow onto my underwear?
So difficult to feel clean.

DALLASITE

He hasn't forgotten his father, how
that bent man tossed his boyhood away,
the rock collection thrown into the sea.
Nothing was ever good enough.

He trusts the rusted seaweed
searching underneath it now.
The slide of stones cushion his club foot,
massage the pain. His father is

dead, and by the sea, he thinks,
I can do whatever I want. Alone,
he stands on the beach of beloved stones,
considers these sea-trundled treasures

he'll polish, then set
in jeweler's silver—Dallasite
named after these shores,
its lobe of green *pillow lava*

ringed in black and white,
formed beneath deep seas. It is
breccia, broken rock chips fused
by pressure and cold, made whole. This man,

his face alight as rain-glazed rock,
blue eyes adamantine,
hair flattened by wind like dune grass
holding the cliff face from falling.

DEPRESSION MAN

"Ditched, Stalled and Stranded, San Joaquin Valley, California, 1935."
—photograph by Dorothea Lange

How in the hollow face of desperation, the eyes startle—huge and bewildered.
A should-be-young man at a steering wheel going nowhere beneath a tattered
car roof. Fruitless air embalms him, his ears dried pears pushed out by a torn
cloth cap; his shredded denim collar holds the reptilian folds of his throat;
a thin hand grasps something hidden from view on the steering column,
some useless mechanism. But his eyes. Opalescent in this black and white
photograph, eroded deep in the sockets of his dry-riverbed face are the eyes of
all men marooned and calling to his mute brother's keeper.

BALANCE

Salt, bitter, sour, astringent and sweet—the five elements required for a balanced Sri Lankan meal.

The cook rubs her skin with sesame oil
essence of rosemary and lavender
eyes dark as tea
speak of loss, and the will of a river
to wend slowly into sea.

In each dish, salt to taste,
1940, the photograph—
her sepia parents in *Kandy*
mother pregnant in the cane-backed chair,
father beside,
salt of Sri Lankan soil

helped their daughter bear
the death of her young husband—
bitten by a cancer, bitter,
as pickle, cracked coriander,
bitter Sinhalese soldiers.

His death sour as the sweat of a *mahout*
prodding his elephant in the bright heat
to roll in the muddy river,
sour as curried peas
ground to a paste.

Tang of yogurt,
lemon and cucumber
soothe the palate. Pel kavi songs
of loneliness and wonder—
Golden and golden, egrets on the riverbank—
cleanse the heart.

She paints watercolours,
stretches with *asanas* each morning
prepares the ground for sweetness—
cashews in coconut cream,
an orange sunrise,
a widow, the whisper of palms.

UNDERLAY

*The United States supported and in many cases engendered
every right wing military dictatorship in the world after the end
of the Second World War...But you wouldn't know it.*
            —Harold Pinter, Nobel Lecture-Literature 2005

Odd not to have noticed
how the rug
does not fit
in the bedroom where it has been
for twenty years—gold on a painted teal floor,
how it would fit better
in the office
with all those years of its wrong blue carpet
rucked up under
the heavy wheels of a desk chair.
All those years of rumple straightening,
trying to make it work,
believing it did. How odd
not to have woken one morning and seen
something just didn't fit,
accepted the wrongness of it
welcomed the labour of change—
the rolling of rugs, the hauling
the laying anew.
How odd not to have noticed,
not to have wanted to see
the lies, the mismatch
the dirt under the carpet
to have spent so much in blindness.

RITUAL FOR THE WINTER SOLSTICE

The universe sleeps / And its gigantic ear
Full of ticks / That are stars / Is now laid on its paw
　　　　—Mayakovsky

And after the long quiet,
after the stained glass windows
have slumped to black,

we rise and walk into the night,
into the Labyrinth, light
a candle and enter

the outer rim.
Each brick a day, say,
each deliberate step

we circle the year
like a bear padding earth
before bedding down.

We spiral into winter,
its rich slumber,
soft-growing shade,

burrow into winter,
deeper into the black and white of it,
the bones-picked-clean-branch of it

against a brooding sky.
The mornings, dark silk dens
we curl into and dream.

Bless winter
and its quiet work
as our pilgrimage

leads to our wild centre,
the shortest, doused-candle day. And what might we meet?

The minotaur? Trapped fear of wilderness,
groggy demi-god, bleary-eyed and stinking.
And what if

this time we do not kill what we fear,
but make peace,
hold out our hairless hand for its paw

to allow the stumble, each brick, each brick
as the Labyrinth releases us,
and we lift our damp noses and sniff.

APPROACH

And God said, Let us make man in our image...and let them have
dominion... over all the earth, and over every creeping thing that
creepeth upon the earth.
    —Genesis 1:26

Approach nature as you would a horse on a morning dew-licked field,
bend your head; take on the horse's shape, its flicky energy.

Let the blood nicker through your veins, your hundred pounds
to its thousand. Yet know that you will put the hard

bit into its soft mouth. Will heave your commanding
body onto its back. Having so often missed the mark,

relearn to take the horse's cue for direction,
sink into its curve, and yet sit upright.

Man poised on a threshold, flawed and lucent link
between Heaven and Earth, just three finger breadths apart.

II

Tattoo

TATTOO

I believe in motherhood,
though I didn't at the time,
coming after the cookie-cutter mothers
of the fifties, I was the generation
who wanted fancy careers.
I believe bodies can have other plans:
I bore a baby who reminded me
of animal love
from the moment she nursed my blue milk—
a January sun watercolouring her lips
clamped to my untried nipples,
the nubs I'd toughened,
towel-rubbed and burnished
in hard summer light for her.
But I didn't write many praise poems.
I was so tired
trying to be a model mother
in a modern career. I don't believe
in regret, but I do it all the time.
Can we go back and rewrite ourselves? Please.
I believe in self-expression;
but I don't believe in tattoos,
something about poison under the skin
and never being naked again.
I believe in holding on and letting go,
agreeing to disagree, and
that my daughter has the right
to tattoo her beautiful back
in a dragon and a phoenix
because she believes in the swirl
of Yin and Yang and in rising
from the ashes. I believe in life,
though I'm not sure it's everlasting.
I'd like to believe it is,
as strongly as the blue-eyed

painter I met one October,
his frescoes shouting angels from the ceiling,
resurrection from the walls in vermilion and silver,
lapis and gold. Shining, shining. I believe
in colour, in what I see before me—
the sharp desert light
how it cuts hills pink and sawdust yellow,
and in the raven, its huff
of wing as it black-beats its way
across a blue sky. I believe
in saying the unsaid:
my father wanted a son,
someone to whom he could teach the trumpet.
I sat for hours at a piano bench with Mrs. Ma
who rapped my fingers and told me
I wasn't good enough.
I believe I knew that already;
I understood the seen and the unseen.
And in the corridors of the unseen,
did I murder something in my daughter
that day my monstrous impatience
cut her baby fingernails
until her waving finger buds bled?
We commit murders both large and small
and crave forgiveness for them.
Life breathes fire, and spirals
shiny-scaled toward life.
The phoenix feeds on cinnamon,
aromatic spikenard, and myrrh,
immolates and rises crimson
from the ashes,
and our truths are emblazoned
on the backs of our children.

AT THE BEACH

My children spill from the car like herrings
sluiced from a bucket, sheened from back-seat heat.
I school across road these shiny fingerlings
and plant in the sand their water-pale feet.
I peel off coral culottes, yellow tops;
squealing merfolk, their sturdy arms raised
float and sway like anemone on rocks.
Freed, they run naked to sea's lick, and wave
while I sink to towel, bones like ice cream
under sun. In the café kitchens, blue
mussels scrubbed of their anchoring threads, brim
tin pails. I scan for points of my heart's hue—
    like Seurat's bather, they cup hand to mouth,
    into the luminous silence, they shout.

FIRST SIMILE

After rain, isotopes
found in the teeth
of the Amesbury Archer

a rain map from the bite
of this Bronze Age immigrant—
found near Stonehenge but bone-quenched

from a central European creek. After rain,
in Hardy's Wessex on the cusp
of the industrial, a traveller sips

from a sudden stream, tips face
to sooty sunbeam, blind
to the coal-covered bark, the extinction

of the pale peppered moth. After rain,
acid burns holes in stone,
drains clog with candy wrappers,

and oil rainbows slide slick to the sea.
In a winter storm, my child runs
in the rain

on the windy deck
of his first ferry boat ride, and shouts,
The rain is like needles on my face.

SMALL SIN

Forgive yourself

that time walking down steep stairs
your daughter's tiny hand let slip,

the fall.

DRIVING OUT OF THE WOODS ON CANADA DAY

Here we are with our two plump ones dozing in their car seats coming back from the cabin in the woods—no electricity, no running water, just a lake pristine and buddha-serene. Two sunlit days asplash, three black and silent nights, holy darkness unpunctured by street lamp, cedar trees blanketing our slumber. But now we return to the city, muscles seizing slightly for re-entry when off in the distance, an explosion. My husband and I gasp in unison, quick turn to find each other's eyes until another flare makes mirth and afterwards admit we had no idea they were fireworks, thought it was the bomb finally dropped. How the dark threat crouches within, leaps in a thousand coloured lights.

ANTI-VIGILANT MOTHER

Because she'd pile-driven her leg
into his chest and I caught
him chasing her
with a kitchen knife, fur
flying like that time
Pembroke, our pinstriped cat,
fought to protect his food bowl
from the neigbourhood raccoon,
I thought: there is a reason
the first murder in the season of man
was between siblings.

THE GAME WE PLAYED

My daughter sleeps until noon
bangs the door at 2 each night when she comes in
from the bar, smelling of smoke. Her eyes
empty as the beds she makes at her job.

What was that game we played
the two of us in the bathtub?
A game where we submerged
something, searched for it,
plunged the yellow ducky (no, that wasn't it)
under the bubbled bath water? Cheeks flushed
we'd shriek I want my
and name the thing each time
wanting whatever it was we kept drowning.

After a hard day of play group
she'd learned how to draw within the lines,
how not to smack back, but in the tub
I let her be a monster.
I want my

Ah yes: goggles,
that's it,
something to help us see underwater.

ACCIDENTS WHILE DAYDREAMING

1. Concrete

I've descended to the concrete breakwater,
curved and sliding to the edge of the sea.
It's getting dark, a wind coming up.
I'm writing in my head of cinnamon
and sassafras, rubies and sugar.
Mist all day. A veil of fine algae
clings to the slippery sides.
One second, I'm on land; the next
neck deep in winter waves.
My down jacket and high gumboots
fill with ocean. No one is around.
I try to haul myself up onto the slick
cement, easy as climbing a mirror.
To my right: stairs I swim towards;
until mind clicks in. Not with a line
of verse, this time, but with a logical
proposition: if stairs go only from street
to top of breakwater then I cannot reach
them. I stop swimming and bob.
Boots kicked off, sock feet finning.
Tide's advancing. How long
'til hypothermia sets in?
Thirty minutes or three?
Is my brain starting to freeze?
Soon, I'll be seeing palm trees. All the pretty fishies...

2. Goalposts

I'm jogging around the soccer field
across from my house, after a day
of dirty diapers, blue jam smeared on walls,
projectile vomiting from my youngest,

his great gag reflex. I'm panting
with ambition: imagine myself onstage;
a standing ovation for such good mothering.
I close my eyes to better visualize,
have not noticed the goal posts
ahead of me, solid as children.
I'm flat on my back. A stunned bird,
I lie a long time in the indifferent grass,
swinging in the hammock of knotted ground.
My husband at home ices my eye, and
our babies puff my bruised cheek.

3. Dreaming and Driving

I've seen a picture of a hacienda in Mexico,
am traveling there as rain sheets
the windshield of my heavy Ford truck.
Bougainvillea replaces ivy; bright
white plaster, the grey buildings,
and a sapphire pool winks. I hit
the gold Mazda in front and below,
get out and note his bent fender,
his wavy white hair and,
as we stoop to inspect the damage,
the freckle on the back of his neck.

4. Out of the ocean

It's embarrassing to call for help.
Tide and wind are against me,
and I can't make it to the beach.
My first cry is wobbly, but lusty by the third.
Two male joggers leap the seawall—slip
and land on top of me.
We shake hands, I forget
their names, but with the push
of one, I heave myself

onto the shoulders of the other,
flop on the concrete like a dead fish
slapped on a drain board.
Two more joggers tiptoe above the algae,
reach from their sensible place and pull us out.
We stand wet and awake in the windy dark.
I thank them all. Someone asks
if I need a ride home.
No, I say, I just live over there,
cross the road and pad
into Ross Bay cemetery,
wet-sock feet
careful among the graves.

FUGITIVES FROM THE MOTHER-DAUGHTER WAR ZONE, WE DRIVE FROM SEA TO SKY

I dress in the dark, prod my daughter awake;
we haul skis, board, and boots out to the truck.
North up Capilano Road. The slow sun
of morning dissolves the flicker of street
and bathroom bulb. Highway 99 Sea to Sky,
a day so sharp you could cut your tongue on it.

We swoop in and out of safe conversation.
Before Brackendale, a broad stretch of sea.
A red tugboat tied to a wooden pier,
sharp blue chop of ocean; slivered mountains
beyond, drizzled in white. First stop Squamish—

a decaf soya latte for me,
for her a double espresso. Up
the curving road to Whistler, we slip
to the packed gondola, fly high above
our past and clatter out. Feel our first

tentative wings sliding to the ride
called Seventh Heaven, a moonscape of rock,
bent firs and snow on top of the sunlit world—
the air so clear it's dizzying,
the ring of mountains personal.

I watch her ski ahead of me, wonder
at her going, whether she'll fall
will rouse herself, will quit. She waits
at the crest of the next hill. She's by turns

sensitive and raging, knows the bombed-out
heart I brought to motherhood. Did she think
it was her fault? The way we lurch
from one hormonal mogul to the next;

the sting that time we slapped
each other's faces,
her door slammed so hard
white paint-chips fell.

And what of nature,
the way a person is? I ski toward
her. Rock, snow,
spring melt.

PLACE SETTING

I rage at my teenage son—
this creature stirring for a song—
faces inches apart   he slaps

palm into plaster wall and slams out the door.
The house shakes, the frail glass panels
hold themselves from shattering.

I pace winter-wet streets   remember
how he tore me when born, how
I rocked our blue boy—

child asking now
for another mother,
one who'll let him go.

I return and make a carrot cake, complicated
by raisins and grated apple folded in.
I lay place mats while it bakes,

leave it to cool, leave
the porch light on.
In the night I hear his heavy tread,

the pull of guitar string,
a tune he knows I hum.
Morning and he enters the kitchen

I drizzle honey into cream cheese
spread it thick as perseverance,
smooth as consolation. He pours us

orange juice, digs out dessert forks.
We sit by big windows
in the rinsed light and eat.

KASPAROV

These machines are training us; we're coming along well,
my driving companion says as he pushes the CD
into the player a second time. It spits the disk out again;
he pushes back and so it goes.

Chess grandmaster Kasparov ponders strategy
against Deep Junior, the world's reigning
supercomputer. Kasparov faces a machine
for the first time since his loss
to IBM's Deep Blue in '97.
The computer has shown it has great problems
with the black pieces, he says.

My son emails me his essay from a Toronto tower.
It's due tomorrow. A paper on Mencius, his philosophy
of Goodness and Evil in Man. Mencius says,
the feeling of commiseration is what we call Humanity;
the feeling of shame and dislike is what we call Righteousness;
the feeling of respect and reverence is what we call Propriety;
and the feeling of right and wrong is what we call Wisdom.
These he calls the Four Beginnings.
Ancient wisdom wired.

The woman attacked and screaming
in the back lane of her city,
unaided by neighbours who thought
they were hearing someone's TV,
could not believe what they were seeing:
virtual reality deletes all Four Beginnings.

Kasparov makes a brilliant move
to get Deep Junior out of the book,
force it to think on its own.
Deep Junior is so confounded
it goes on screensaver.

Seems there's one sure way
for man to beat machine: act a little crazy.

Our family cabin in the woods
without electricity or running water.
We've left Douglas fir to grow,
been told we're foolish not to develop.

Stags slow-prance through salal
to drink from the lake. Sun spills from their lips.
We sleep in cedar and blackness heals.
Days and the green forces leaf into us.

A Tokyo man visits and cringes
at the water snakes and dragonflies he is sure
are going to kill him. Raised in a tower,
nursed on screens, and fed computer chips,
he'll design the cities in which I cannot live.

Here we work in pen and paper.
From a lamp-lit window,
cheer Kasparov on.

In the city, I edit with red pen,
send my son's essay across the continent
via scanner, type-talk to him on MSN.
Cn u read it? ttyl ☺
He'll email the second draft
before he catches the subway to class,
morning for him, 2:30 my time;

he'll call on the cell tonight,
c'mon, c'mon
ah, when will I touch his face again?

TEACH THEM TO BE BLIND

Stay to lunch, we say to our daughter. She
takes a tin of tuna from the cupboard
while we discuss the deception of the jerk
at the towing company who won't see
he punched a hole in her car; instead he
meets the questions of our gentle daughter
with blind silence. Happy that he caught her.
We each fix something different, for me
soup; you like cheese, toast bread for sandwiches.
I wash and spin-dry organic lettuce.
She lifts the tin says, *Isn't this loaded
with mercury?* We don't respond because
    we don't want her to eat it. Yet here
      it is in our home waiting to be eaten.

III
Leaving the Body

LEAVING THE BODY

In the dream my mother has it all organized,
but I can't follow her instructions.
I go from the bedroom to tell my cousin,
who is entertaining guests,
How did she die? she asks.
We all die in pieces, I reply.
From the kitchen, I phone my sister.
I say, I guess I should call an undertaker.
My sister agrees that I should do something.

*

Walking through the cemetery, I see Mr. Ryan's grave.
Family has left red-berried pyrocanthus for Christmas
and green pine boughs to circle its perimeter,
a paper maple planted in the centre
so they can write messages on the peeled bark.
When he died in his own bed,
his daughter wanted to hold the body,
until she felt he was really gone,
but a daughter-in-law would not hear of it,
called the ambulance, had the body carried away.

*

A couple sailing on a Pacific passage
ran into trouble with a tangled halyard.
The husband tied himself to the mast,
his wife winched him up to the spreader.
He untied and retied himself higher still
had a heart attack and died.
She could not get him down,
motored through the Doldrums
for three weeks
while birds feasted,

ate the eyes. Under the hot moon
his flesh dripped like candle wax onto the deck.

*

My friend flew across the country
to be with her father dying on the family farm.
All the siblings came from away, except one.
The daughter who'd stayed
lay across the foot of their father's bed
as he shriveled like a snowberry
from white to papery brown;
she guarded him, vigilant,
determined to peel the pyjamas,
sponge the thin arms and chest. Lick the legs and toes
with a warm cloth and give a long last stroke
to his back.

*

Suicide tourists travel to die
with a group called Dignitas.
Mr. Crews from Liverpool flies
to Zurich, his last act
to sway public opinion back home.
His own country won't hasten his death,
though they know his disease is terminal,
the pain constant.
A tableau—his wife and son on either side
of the bed. The weight of drugs
lifts suffering, slows heart
loosens eyelids. He feels
his wife's familiar palm,
his son's steady hand,
a bridge for the crossing.

*

On my last visit, before his fatal heart attack,
my father stood on the spring street
waving as I drove away. His Falstaffian body
grew smaller and smaller in my rear-view mirror,
until I turned a corner,
and he vanished
in the morning sun.

AT THE WAVECREST RESORT

My white thigh under the sheet
skin cool and glassy as the southern Pacific
on this calm winter morning   but within

the body eroding
as the lava'd cliffs of Molokai
rain-carved.

In a bowl by the bed   plumeria
I've plucked from a resident tree

white flower   flesh-petalled
thick-flushed yellow from throat
pales at the tip

from a sturdy lime stem
uprush of sweet lemon.

The mirror in the bedroom reflects my mother's face
its brave thinness

this perfume lasts only as long
as a sharp pull of breath.

AND STILL I GO TO CALL HER EVERY SUNDAY

On the day my mother falls from a stroke,
I come running to her bedside
hear her half-stilled, one-sided farewell
while the other side soldiers on
until the family gathers;
from a lucid voice deep-buried,
she gives blessings: my beautiful girls,
my favorite guy, give a hug
loving and after all loved.
Her flesh itches, muscles entombed
I roll her flaccid body and stroke,
cream-smooth the crumpled sheets of skin,
cradle her while bruised rains fall.
She calls to Uncle Jim, dead at fourteen,
I whisper wondered greetings to the other side.

PRIMARY COLOURS

Why did I leave you
even once in that hospital bed
frozen in a coma in the white room
and go to the Chagall exhibit at the gallery?

Women floating over houses
blue, red   that yellow.
Did you know the young mourning gecko
is a genetic replica of her mother? These days

I watch her move toward a spider's web
strung in a corner of the porch,
still her nictitating membrane,
perceive the whole fly caught, its sunlit blue,

the yellow spokes of net. And tonight
how I wish upon these stars—long-gone and gold—
to still the third eyelid the next time
I meet death   be unblind to its colours.

WEARING MY MOTHER'S DRESSES

Thou art thy mother's glass, and she in thee
Calls back the lovely April of her prime.
　　　　　—William Shakespeare, "Sonnet 3"

At your funeral, I wore the chocolate cocktail dress
tied at the waist with the rolled cord;
sis chose one of your beaded sweaters;
Auntie Claire, the navy suit—

a tribute to your walk-in closet,
how you tailored your girls
in yellow gingham sprung wide with crinolines,
velvet smocks with white collars,
elbow-length gloves, blue-sashed dancing frocks.

Your red ballroom gown,
heavy silk with beaded bodice,
I'll sheath in cleaner's plastic, hold on to.

I fit the mocha lace
A-line, the one scalloped at the hem.

I'll throw parties just to wear it.

Remember the green and white floral number,
how its wide skirt taffeta-shushed as you passed me
getting ready to go out? I'd follow you,
bury my jammy face in its glossy folds

and when you were gone, I'd sneak
into your cupboard

clomp in your pink velveteen heels,
silver brocade dress,
swing a stole around my shoulders.
In your full-length glass,
watch myself twirl: embroidered stars, black shot silk.

RIDING THE BUS TO DIALYSIS

She clutches the handrail down the few steps
to the shuttle arrived to take her
on these tri-weekly trips to the hospital.
For the past five years. She carries a light
supper of sandwich and apple.
I've asked if she wants me to come but
she senses my reluctance, tells me to stay.
She's in a conversation with her seatmate
as the bus pulls away. At a cocktail party
again, Hong Kong, June, 1969—in a lace
brocade suit. A beaded purse dangles
from her slim arm. In her hand, rye
whiskey and water. How they laugh, how
often I ride that bus in my dreams.

YOUR DISAPPEARING ACT

When I saw you naked in the bathroom,
the sparse grey patch between your legs frightened me.
I didn't know it went grey and vanishing.
Who wants to know that much future?

Crystal ball in your back of bumps,
scabs and skin flaps you ask me to moisturize.
I spread the cream over your dry map,
think of contours blurring since your fifties—

the day you came home from your library job
to report that the men no longer flirted
when it was your turn at the front desk—
your disappearing act going on for years.

Funny, how the more the body disappears,
the more we pay attention to it.
Those last years spent in careful steps,
eating, sleeping, filing the body's statements—

all that ordering in the chaos
of pumps and tubes. A compass
needed to find oneself. But know this:
I see you more than when you were here,

still think how I traced shoulder ridges,
and bumped my fingers down
your thinning ribs—corporeal memory
growing heavy on my spine.

ONE HUNDRED AND THREE

Everyone forgets that the world lies scattered
under an old man's chin, chest caved in,
eyes closed over his newspaper. We keep forgetting
it wouldn't work to expect him to grow young
again, come dancing, raise a pint at the pub.
On the other side of life, he is still breathing,
sedate as marble, or raging at the nurses, and at his son
whose fault, he's certain, this ageing is. And he thinks
some days you're his dead brother, or his savior, either way,
you never come often enough. Anyone can tell you
it's over, or it isn't. He waits in the empty hallway,
lingers on a bed behind a curtain.
At least he loves the sparrows that light
upon the plastic feeder dish, the tip
and spill, the squabbling for seed.
That the indifferent sky understands
is an odd comfort as we wheel him
along the sea, his gloved hands grip
the blanket slipping from his knees,
his face fixed on the horizon. No one
has come back to tell him anything.

I COULD NOT FIND A POEM FOR THE DYING

How tulips begin hard-waxed
upright, tight-cupped, bright pink and white—

then slow-swoop over time toward gravity.
Green stems swan-necked. Lush petal heads

turn a dust pink, or sheer white,
their edges desiccated and curled.

A corolla of six: two persistent
petals skyward; the rest sweeping

stunned beyond
the vase's vitreous blue.

Do they feel pain as a desiring
that ushers toward release?

I change their water, watch them lift awhile
like that day when you felt hollowed out

in an utter efflorescence of illness
and how the lilt of a friend's fresh voice,

a hand gracing your spine,
brought a brief return.

YOU CAME HOME

Because you had trouble speaking Japanese
after thirty years of living there. Because
hope is a tyrant and salt water a kind of blood.
Because they'd done everything they could
and your sister had prepared a bed
in her island living room where clouds
smudged the windows, pillowed
the distant hills. Because your sister
could talk about funerals, and
your husband did not leave his work. Because
your mouth was last—bread, please,
peaches, a slice of pear—
and your stomach had become a shy animal.
Because even home took on
a foreign tongue; you
tucked into the passenger seat
staring, through the dusk-washed windshield
at the valley of fat sheep. Because
even what we know is a surprise.

HOW YOU FALL A LITTLE BIT IN LOVE

with the blue-eyed writer who reminds you of your son
whose eyes are hazel, actually, and he lives
far away, both the writer and the son.

And what about your boyfriend falling in love
over lunch with your mother?
The graceful way she poured the tea,
serving your future together light in his cup.

How often you meet your daughter overseas—
that tour through the Tuscan vineyard
her informative talk beside the oaken casks, pouring
a glass of Chianti reserve, sneezing slightly from spring pollen.
How you wanted to gather this bella in your arms
pass her a clean handkerchief.

You saw your lost father, today, parking a car
close to where you were going; he'd driven around and around,
just as you had with your dear friend at the wheel,
both peering through the windshield,
to find the perfect spot.

And you a little in love with that young woman
who reminds you of your mother, makes you wonder
if at the moment of your mother's passing,
their lungs billowed,
a shared dove-sweetness exhaled.

Why did your black lab flatten herself only
for the neighbourhood carpenter in an ecstasy
of reunion? You almost believed in past lives
as he bent to scratch his happiness
to see her again. The spark of love
rolling her over and over in the damp grass.

IV

In the Night Sky, A Crab

BLUEBERRIES

Mr. Davis calls every May when the pewter rains lift
to ask how many pounds. When I see him
in the hospital TV room, we're both hooked to IV's.
He is thin-skulled, veins pop cobalt in his extended hand.
The air between us smells of ammonia and a sweet rot.
We're swathed in bleached gowns. The morphine drip transcends
but does not eradicate the pain—making Buddhists of us all.
And here it is May, Mr. Davis, berry man,
harbinger of spring is cloistered in the next room
amid trays of grey meat, plastic cups of tinned fruit,
sealed windows that block the birdsong.

CANCER COUNTRY

Aligned body alone in a bright room,
the only sound metallic bleat
of a ray gun as it circles the sacrificed

of what? Canaries in the coal mine;
there but for the grace of God go—
statistical probability, taking one for the team.

And what is my response/ability?
Have I immigrated or been abducted
to this continent? I am undecided

how much to embrace its customs.
Its language foreign, a dire vocabulary:
stromal invasion, oophorectomy, path of the disease.

The lick of beads on a chilled wine glass,
the cram-my-cheeks-at-the-buffet days
now gone. What can this country teach me?

I surrender to weekly meditation sessions
bathe in flutes and wind chimes.
Hello life, says a girl in pale robes, *hello.*

AFTER SURGERY

I am not to lift
anything over ten pounds. At birth
my daughter neared this weight.
Each day of my recovery,
I remember the heft
of my firstborn, her first home
no longer there.

IN THE NIGHT SKY, A CRAB

I

I have crossed over.
Adrift in this swollen constellation,
my universe.

II

In the night sky, a crab.
Clusters buried in the bodies of clouds
divide like cells, multiply.
Because Cancer failed to defeat Hercules,
the gods did not give it bright stars.

III

The sailboat tips in a blast
of mist-laden wind. Sudden seawater,
its insistent lick brings me to life again.
A moment for a moment forgetting.

IV

The miner breathes asbestos for breakfast.
Sixty years later, he eats a piece of his lung.

V

What illness teaches us:
the soft dark at the back of the eyelid,
so much to see.

VI

How one miner is afflicted, another is not.
Why cells move from bud to blight,
and hope, like a zephyr,
breathes healing.

VII

My brittle heart cracked open
to the kindness of friends—
ripe fruits in brimming baskets.

VIII

I walk in the graveyard
where everything is greener—
moss caresses white marble,
red carnations sigh,
and fling themselves down in the rain.
The mushroomed air smells of birth.

IX

So much red:
a womb entombed.

X

At the diagnosis: a stab;
inner scream. Ask me
what it sounds like:
under a blanket of snow,
vole listening to the red fox.

XI

Unslept night.
I soak in the morning chitter:
want to know the names of birds.

XII

How even though bombs explode,
civilians go to the grocery store.

XIII

Spring summer fall—
cells like hydrangea
blue and deep pink.

TEACUP

Rinsed and tipped on its saucer blue and gold
it dries on the counter. Beside the rim,
small pool of water, tea-stained, and cold
I quick wipe, remembering father's trim
finicky kitchen ways when he grew ill.
No puddles on his counters, and steady
caffeine cups to replenish strength's slow spill.
I'm home too—felled by the fluid body's
capriciousness. He is lost to me.
Ashes in an urn I talk to, leavings
in a cup. I understand now why he
filled his porcelain days with bright cleaning:
        polishing the silver through winter's rain,
        calling on his vessel to scrub its veins.

BETWEEN TREATMENTS

In a field, the heavy sleeping of things—
the cedars, the naked maples, tucked roots of roses;
in the bay, black rocks, their scattered bulk
reclines in a sea smooth as sheet metal.
I listen to the duck's complaint,
to the muffled moan of geese as they fly
invisible in a heron-feather sky. Snow
weights the boughs of pine,
thick-paints a group of backyard chairs;
snow wraps the red arbutus in white silk,
brings light to evening walks.

If Winter lacks compassion, why
drop diamonds on my dark glove?

OLD PHOTOGRAPHS

What to do with photographs mute in drawers
and damp basements. I could
set up a card table in an empty room,
scrounge ten shoeboxes—
one for each neglected year—
peer into matte faces,
try to date them.
Outside my window, mynah birds
pluck at grass, oil-rig heads
pumping the dirt.
Their banana-yellow beaks
know what to do.

Two neighbours and I have cancer—
frail bald chicks.

We consider our options:
put photos in fat albums,
record? Or
scour the earth,
pluck bugs from winter thaw.

AN ORDINARY DAY

Pelvic brachytherapy is used as the final treatment
and delivers radiation directly inside the vaginal vault.

When the nurses strap my calves into stirrups,
I say I'm ready to ride. The doctor
slips in a Plexiglas dildo,
and I ask my size, *ordinary, you are
just ordinary*, he quips then comes round
to squeeze my shoulder before he leaves, before
they all leave me with the chest-high machine,
sheathed in white porcelain. The ray gun's green
and red lights circle like a carousel.
Beyond the partition, I hear the nurses
discuss the casseroles they will make for dinner
while my radioactive lover burns me:
its eyes just blink and blink.

APPOINTMENT WITH THE SPECIALIST

I ask you to come with me this time
not to drive or clothe or feed,
I am capable of all that. I ask
you to hold my hand. Just
that and perhaps laugh with me
in the waiting room.
I know you have to change your plans,
to come with me was not on your list,
with its import, its grab on the world,
the whirly-twirly list I lived on.
Please, be with me
for awhile, let me tell you
something I've not admitted,
words I've been meaning to say
for some time. Words that fill
like warm resin,
rise from root to limb
to leafy throat.

And you, so used to my thick bark,
my gnarled independence.
But now. My skin worn as vellum.

Read to me a child's story,
the one where the mother finds her girl,
no matter where she hides.

SWIMMING AT THE OAK BAY REC.

I thread into blue
arms stitch open the closing

my head like a needle up and down
mouth swallowing skeins of silken air

the swimmer in front's retreating feet
undulate like seals behind a silver scrim of bubbles

at the turn of the lane her black-suited bottom rises
white strip of thigh sparkles then springs off the concrete wall

the man we pass wallows like a loaded boat
we're racing but he doesn't know it

I goggle him below the surface a kind of elegance
his trunks flutter loose like butterfly fish

at each cool round I glimpse the guards footed to the pool deck
the swimmer to them like Melville's porpoise

plows aqua in huzzahs of froth
unleashing the body's lust for movement

an old woman's crutches lean on a silver handrail
in the shower her slumped waist and blue veined legs

ankles swollen puffer fish
but the pool knew her wet body whole

and after our swim soaped and rinsed
shiny as mackerel we are

ecstatic trout dimpling lake water
kissing the surface at dawn.

AFTERNOON TV

John of God is a farmer in Brazil and the sick, dressed in muslin bring their illnesses like garlands. They stand against a white-washed wall. John baptizes a cotton wad, reams their noses—like red earth, blood drops fall; he touches the bowed heads of his followers, their knees crumpling in an ecstasy of hope. And if they die, at least they die like cliff climbers reaching for a hold. A summer morning, a convert whose cancer was terminal back home hikes from a valley into Brazilian sky. All these miraculous years later, his footprints grooved in the dust. What is this mystery of healing? It seeps from John, sustains like locust and honey—taste of the will to live, unfathomable.

CANCER CLINIC: HEALING TOUCH SESSION, 2:30 THURSDAYS

Priestesses of the unseen, your hands
hover just above the flesh, yet burrow
heat and healing deep to the marrow.

How you unlatch fists, and gather pain,
soothe with polished light.
Would we once have burned you at the stake?

We lie here now and laud you—
gleaners who clean energy fields,
who bend to the task, fill aprons

with suffering's stubbled waste.

UNDER THE LUMBER, WHITE GRASS

Another sparrow trapped in the unfinished room;
the birds keep seeking a place to roost,
fluttering through a gap between wall and new roof.

I hear the thud of their feathered chests
against wood-framed window panes, and rush
to release them from this particular death.

Impossible to live without killing something.
Don't panic, I assure them, opening
the windows wide. This is not your home.

Fly away. Porcelain skull crazed,
dazed in the snowberry's winter twigs,
and a falcon in the spruce.

THE WORD I WANT TO HEAR

A chest x-ray, my clavicle bone
swan wing in the body's grey sky
upsweep and swoop. The white heart cupped
between breast lines perfect and pencil thin.

I scan for dark smudges and find none.
Probe the technician for the word I want to hear.
Lovely, I say, *is this?*   *And this?*
And still   she won't say

slaps the second picture on her light screen
and we study a profile. The spine's "s"
a swan's neck each vertebra glides into the next
and again, the heart, its cloudy mass

dominates. And the technician knows
her kindness overcomes her, or perhaps it is the truth.
My finger prods the emptiness of lung
Normal, she says,   *it looks normal.*

EARTH MOTHER HYSTERECTOMY

In Emergency, when the gynecologist (a confident man who'd
misdiagnosed) said nothing would be different without her ovaries,

she shouted: *How'd you like it if I cut off your balls?*
Not the best thing to say to someone with a knife in his hand.

Her husband, rolling his eyes, squeezed her thigh,
the sheets beneath her ironed with blood.

She won the first round, saved the womb but didn't solve
the problem. In the end, it was a complete rout.

What does the loss of a womb mean,
and its ovaries? Centre of creativity, kundalini severed.

She sees a healer who says even without some parts,
we can be whole. He plows his palms into her pelvic bowl,

tills her energy fields and redirects diverted rivers
to find the power of that lost flow again. And the spirit

does compensate, finds in defeat a subtle strength;
but, let's set the record straight: it is different,

she says, dry now the desertified canal, sperm boats
stranded like the tilted fishing fleet of the Aral Sea.

I USED TO WONDER WHEN HAPPINESS
WOULD COME

It comes the way the door to the coffee shop
swings out to spring sunshine
and how the man
holds it open for the man behind

in the way my daughter runs up the steps
stops to sniff   blue hyacinth in the hallway

in a long distance phone call
on a Saturday afternoon
my mother's voice   my ear
her ear   my voice

hums in the dial tone chant
of Tibetan monks
their egg-yolk robes
scarlet sashes against a white wall

comes again in the silky decay
multi-hued   open-petalled
of red tulips

with the finch
alighting
on a winter-bare branch

happiness charges the room
as a wide-eyed child leaping on the bed,
lifting the hooded lids of late night drinkers.

SNOWY OWL ON A SUBURBAN STREET

White wings split the night
never real until now.
Subconscious owl   wise bird of the fairy tale.

It's as if Jack had climbed down from a green vine
as if Alice had popped out of the sewer line
or the lamppost opened into Narnia.

Ghost owl you're like the Arctic,
something I've never seen
but need to know is there,
that space   that whiteness.

Athena's lunar bird   reflective thought
Native night bird   conductor of shades
to the grave. You feel like a warning

a visitation from the gods
for our bruised home
always now the end of the world
glaciers calving into rivers of melt.

Yet when you lift off the dark line,
fly inches above our heads
your body angel-bright
we feel blessed.

I CARRY THIS BODY AROUND

*...it is no longer regarded as an accomplishment
to know how to die gracefully at dawn.*
—Flambeau in "Father Brown"

Mornings, I muck out the stalls
at Mary's stable. Cart away
the laden sawdust and sweep;
rake fresh red ground and yellow feed,

fill the water bucket half-full.
All the while, a splendid cock
struts the corridor, grubs for bits,
cockadoodles when the mood strikes,

or flutters to perch on a wooden wall.
I lift my gaze to him and beyond
to the pasture where the horses graze,
to the green hills purpling as dusk comes on.

At a whistle, the horses race from field
to fresh hay. I trot to each door, open for Arrow,
the Dutch Warmblood; Buddy, the Thoroughbred,
and for Snowfall; thrill of a full-grown horse

galloping towards my frailty.
Snowfall slows at his stall and Arrow leans,
attempts a nip at his neighbour's haunch—
aliveness of a body biting into air

is how I want to feel,
when every final morning dawns—
graceful and unafraid
to bite each innocent day.

BUG

Natura Devroans; Natura Devorata

Tiny bug, you breathe the blue of my shirt;
then traverse its striped field
to pink and green. Do you see its colour?
Your body no bigger than a spot of flung
ink, paper wings a diminuendo
of the dragonfly's. In a world of wasps,
of voracious ducks with their crushing bills
and the trout's dusk feed, peace is brief.

You tickle my stomach's brown beach
and the vulture, high above, sees the spot
we are, plowing its relentless circle. Gold
above the bird, the sun devouring.

A YEAR AND A HALF

She runs a sushi café
makes neat packets of rice
red pepper, avocado slice
pale mounds of veined shrimp.

She has a year and a half
to live, the doctors say.

She goes out for a cigarette break
between radiation treatments
allows her man to get drunk
fall apart, call her cunt.
Says he's OK when he's sober.

She doesn't want to read
about her illness, or
even talk about her body;
demands it buck up, be tough,
hang in until a cure;

yet here in her shop
when she hears I've had cancer,
she comes around the counter
gives a hug, a soft word,
pink and naked.

ROOM 1311, BUCERIAS, ONE YEAR AFTER TREATMENT

Here, even air
is wet and hot   the sea
blood-warm,
clothing   filmy.

After two days,
skin darkens
to bikini line   startles
makes white flesh
more private.

This afternoon   we lie
you and I
naked on the king canvas
doze like geckos

watch columns of sun
through partly-opened drapes
undulate.

Beyond the palms   surf
crests the shore   pulses
and the mood shifts like light.

Your finger traces my collar bone
slides to pelvic bowl
with its gleam of proud flesh
where the scalpel cut
its blue
radiation tattoo.

Orange light scrawls rust walls,
and I lift   to your memory of me.

I FIRST MET GOD AT O'HARE AIRPORT

I was lying on the hard plastic benches
molding myself to a sleep that would not come;
bumped from one flight, hoping for the next,
under fluorescent moons, we talked all night.
I was nineteen, on my way to New Orleans,
He was wrinkled. I don't remember
anything we said, just the joy of it:
He kept me company, swept cigarette butts.

The next time She breezed through in a dream,
no kidding—gliding down a stone pier
on her way to a round plaster chapel. Tall,
slim, white-robed under a cobalt blue sky,
her path lit by stars so close we could touch them.
That summer, I lived on Crete,
in sad love with a cruel man.
She didn't speak, just led me
into her glorious womb-chapel,
candle-lit, wax-gilded,
bade me stay.

And that winter in Montreal,
foolish girl, I left the bar with a man
in a long fur coat. His empty apartment
where a party was supposed to be.
The metal click of medicine cabinet,
crinkle of the condom cracked open,
his free arm holding me down
on the dark bed. Spilled
onto the street at 3 a.m., I stood
in the glazed orange city: its silence.
I hailed the first car that drove by
and there He was. On the drive to the hostel,
I told God everything.

SAFARI TO THE O'KEEFE HOUSE, GHOST RANCH, NEW MEXICO

She just wants to touch the round
adobe walls of Georgia's house. Get off
this tourist bus. Kneel
beside the salt bush and bend
nose to orange globe mallow, purple aster

for the colour
of where Georgia sipped her solitude
quiet as mule deer from desert springs,
found herself different
from the way they pictured her.

She just wants to feel the dust
coat her face, erode the separation.
The body alone,
independent—
able to see the hills anew.

But the driver won't stop,
only lets them lean out for pictures,
stay a safe distance.
As if the house were a lioness
crouching among the prickly pear.

WHAT WE CANNOT SEE

—from Jean-Simeon Chardin's still life "Jar of Apricots, 1758"

We see domestic bliss, the stillness, the alls-right-with-the-world way
bread crumbs lie on a plain table, the loaf just sliced and eaten,
the way coffee steams from china cups and the silver spoon
tilts not at windmill fantasies. We are real, the objects say,
they exude a comfortable knowing thick as the amber syrup
bathing the plump apricots. Look how the light
comes from above, from the right, through a window we cannot see,
only its sill turquoise against the mud-brown wall. Light glazes it all—
the glossy apricots, the claret partially drunk, even the abandoned orange.
Has a soldier-son been called to his death and his parents
just learn the news? Are the crumbs, the claret, the jarred
fruit reminders of what was? Life before the messenger came
and objects lost all meaning. Grief can drain the joy from apricots,
the sound from the tambourine propped against the wall, leave
the paper package tied with string, unopened. Grief can stop the clock,
as a still life can capture a moment so set in time yet timeless—
crumbs so immediate we can imagine the hand that sawed the bread
just out of view, can hear the clink of coffee cup just set down, breathe its steam.
And joy can stop time, too. Objects blush alive again, eternal—
the scrape of their soldier son's boot upon the door sill,
(his knowing they'd be just about to eat), their uprush as they run to greet him
returned, returned. Faces shiny with relief as they take his greatcoat
from his thin shoulders, stroke his hollowed cheek and usher him to table,
Claret, they'd say, apricots.

IN PRAISE OF MUSHROOMS

My boot almost crushes domed towers dew-beaded,
sprung in the night through loamy ground,
knobbed umber caps on vellum stocks
frilled gills underneath to breathe in the deep.

Mushrooms surprising sprouted bright
white buttons on blackened logs, or fleshy
ruffles from ruin where tub and tiles meet.

Precious fungus—shitake, chanterelle,
oyster, portabella and truffles—
sponge-tongued taste of earth.

Spores float like words,
take hold in the cold and wait
to bloom in the dark.

ACKNOWLEDGMENTS

The poem "Late Summer in Frederick Arm", won the Malahat Review's 2011 Open Season Awards for Poetry. "What We Cannot See" won the 2009 Federation of BC Writers Literary Writes Competition. "The Word I Want to Hear" received honourable mention in the Banff Centre Bliss Carman Poetry Award in 2005. "Good Holding Ground" received honourable mention in the Victoria Writers Society Contest in 2004, and in 2003 "Weeding" placed second in the Arts Angels Online Competition, kick-starting my publication endeavours.

I would like to thank the Banff Centre Wired Writing program for the scholarship it gave me to attend in 2009. My thanks also to the editors of the literary magazines where many of these poems have been published: *The Antigonish Review, CV II, Grain, The Malahat Review, Passages North, Prairie Fire, Room* and *Quills.*

I am most grateful to the poetry tribe for their encouragement, skill and inspiration—especially, The Waywords, former and new—Andrea, Barb, David, Grace, Judith, Karen, Pam and Yvonne; and the more recent FB's—Arleen, Barb, Claudia, Julie, Lisa and Trish. Patricia Young combed through this manuscript in its beginnings and Sue Goyette did the same with a later version, such brilliant editing and teaching from them both. Finally, I would like to thank Patrick Lane who opened the door at the Glenairley retreats, and Wendy Morton who nudged me through. "I Could Not Find a Poem for the Dying" is dedicated to the memories of Joni Mara Willis and Pauline Mara Isserlis. The poem "Wearing My Mother's Dresses" is dedicated to my sister, Diana. My deep gratitude also goes to the doctors who approached with heart as well as skill, especially Elissa McMurtrie, Jim Melling, and Steven Starr, and to the family and friends, ripe fruit in brimming baskets, who were there.

This book is dedicated to Phyllis and Ralph Woodman.

For Justine and Quinn
...more than the sun, the moon and the stars in the sky above.

And for Duncan, such love.

ABOUT THE AUTHOR

Cynthia Woodman Kerkham was born in Toronto, raised in Hong Kong and Vancouver and has lived in France. She has a degree in Asian Studies and English literature from UBC and has worked as a potter, journalist and teacher. Her poems have appeared in many literary journals including *The Antigonish Review*, *Room*, *CV2*, *The New Quarterly*, *The Malahat Review*, *Grain* and *Prairie Fire*. In 2009 she won the Federation of BC Writers Literary Writes Competition, and in 2011 the Malahat's Open Season Awards for Poetry. She lives in Victoria when not sailing the West Coast. *Good Holding Ground* is her debut collection of poems.